Sinnerman

Books by Michael Waters

Sinnerman 2023
Caw 2020
The Dean of Discipline 2018
Celestial Joyride 2016
Selected Poems (UK) 2011
Gospel Night 2011
Darling Vulgarity 2006
Parthenopi: New and Selected Poems 2001
Green Ash, Red Maple, Black Gum 1997
Bountiful 1992
The Burden Lifters 1989
Anniversary of the Air 1985
Not Just Any Death 1979
Fish Light 1975

Edited:

Border Lines: Poems of Migration (with Mihaela Moscaliuc) 2020
Reel Verse: Poems About the Movies (with Harold Schechter) 2019
Contemporary American Poetry (with A. Poulin, Jr.) Eighth Edition, 2006
    Seventh Edition, 2001
Perfect in Their Art: Poems on Boxing from Homer to Ali (with Robert
    Hedin) 2003
A. Poulin, Jr. Selected Poems 2001
Dissolve to Island: On the Poetry of John Logan 1984

It is difficult to imagine poetry could be more finely crafted and compelling than the work of Michael Waters, who has been quietly writing some of the best poetry in the United States for the past three decades.

—Stephan Delbos, *The Prague Post*

The consistency of his work over the past thirty years has contributed greatly to American letters, and his unique voice within the poetry world illuminates, with precision and clarity, the intricate nature of the human condition.

—Esteban Rodríguez, *American Book Review*

Waters seeks to capture the different kinds of negative space which interpenetrate American public life, history, and even the most intimate of moments "between two bodies"—what he calls "the loneliness of two people / together."

—Jonathan Taylor, *The Times Literary Supplement*

A significant American voice...testifies eloquently to the persistence of the lyric in a time and history that would seek to obliterate it.

—John Mann, *World Literature Today*

Waters stands among the best American poets writing today.

—Roberto Bonazzi, *San Antonio Express-News*

He tempers in his latest collection a delight in wit and wordplay with a rigorous prosodic training throughout a long and distinguished career... A voluptuary of style... Michael Waters is the ablest poet of an able generation.

—Floyd Collins, *The Gettysburg Review*

The Dean of Discipline's absorbing subject is the making of art, showing and teaching us a poet's meticulous and raucous devotion so that we gain a sound and sense of how poems are, in fact, created... Waters's work assumes a divine erotic presence even in his most harrowing poems.

—Judith Vollmer, *The Georgia Review*

Sinnerman

Michael Waters

Etruscan Press

Etruscan Press
Wilkes University
84 West South Street
Wilkes-Barre, PA 18766
(570) 408-4546

 Wilkes
University

www.etruscanpress.org

Published 2023 by Etruscan Press
Printed in the United States of America
Cover art: *ANAMNESIS XXXVII*, pastel on paper, 60" x 40," 2008 © Kathleen Holder
Cover design by Carey Schwartzburt
Interior design and typesetting by Todd Espenshade
The text of this book is set in Adobe Caslon Pro.

First Edition

17 18 19 20 5 4 3 2 1

Library of Congress Cataloguing-in-Publication Data

Names: Waters, Michael, author.
Title: Sinnerman / Michael Waters.
Other titles: Sinnerman (Compilation)
Description: First edition. | Wilkes-Barre, PA : Etruscan Press, 2023. |
    Summary: "'Blessed be sin if it teaches men shame,' wrote Georges Benanos. Sinnerman continues Michael Waters' exploration of transgression as a mode of worship in poems that 'delight in wit and wordplay' (The Gettysburg Review) and display 'raucous devotion' while assuming 'a divine erotic presence even in his most harrowing poems' (The Georgia Review)"—Provided by publisher.
Identifiers: LCCN 2022046003 | ISBN 9798985882445 (trade paperback)
Subjects: LCGFT: Poetry.
Classification: LCC PS3573.A818 S56 2023 | DDC 811/.54--dc23/eng/20230103
LC record available at https://lccn.loc.gov/2022046003

Please turn to the back of this book for a list of the sustaining funders of Etruscan
Press.

This book is printed on recycled, acid-free paper.

For, in certain moods, no man can weigh this world without throwing in something, somehow like Original Sin, to strike the uneven balance.
—Herman Melville

Jesus died for somebody's sins,
but not mine.
—Patti Smith

for Mihaela

sin / in full sun

CONTENTS

WINDOW

The not-there where
The sparrow strikes blunt air

Flies no farther
God-thumbed through every feather

Where someone gazes out
Contemplating doubt

Spring pane
Doubly transparent in rain

Summer: always open
Autumn: forked crack /still unbroken

Narrow border
Between breath   and weather

Winter pane
Doubly transparent in cellophane

Night mirror
With coal-fire interior

Where my twin gazes in
Contemplating sin

BROOKLYN WALK-UP

Too often my mother told the story
Of bundling me into the red snowsuit,
Leaving me scarved & ear-flapped,
Zippered to the chin, baby-bootied
Upon the quilted bed
While she wrestled the carriage
Six flights down tenement steps
Only to return to a locked door,
The key nestled in the handbag
Dangling from the inside hook.
A cry like no other rose inside her.
She rushed again down crooked stairs
Out onto Covert Street,
Past the deli & funeral parlor,
All the way around the corner
To the Irving Avenue alley
Where she grasped then climbed—
This new mother—
The fire escape ladder
Rung by icy rung
To reach the first metal landing, then
Clanged upward floor by floor until,
Crouched upon the uppermost grate,
She could see the swollen,
Immobile, doll-shaped pile.
She raised the unclasped window,
Gathered me, grabbed her bag, descended
Once more the six floors to the cold carriage,
Then raced to the Dekalb Avenue BMT
To meet my father home from work.
Wheeled madly, I slept like a bobbing cork.
She never told him how she'd shut me in,

How she'd gazed through glass
At the clump of cloth,
The breathing heap of wool & cotton
For which she'd leapt beyond her measure.
Motherhood had turned uncommon.
Years later she took such pleasure
In repeating the story, that boy
Swathed like an Andean child
Sacrificed on the mountain peak,
Mummified by the dry, glacial winds,
Never to name his executioner,
That boy her favorite version of me.

LONE HYDRANT

The bonnet of the fire hydrant
Resembles a miniature capitol dome,
Though the R. Mutt readymade gleams redly.
Why this hydrant squats in tall grasses
Is another of this village's mysteries.
My father steered the rear end of a hook-and-ladder
Through Brooklyn streets, sometimes
Rumbling down Covert to impress our neighbors.
With a wrench longer than my arm
He'd twist the hydrant's nipple to allow cold water
To arc into the gutter on a fiery noon.
My friends & I took turns dancing in the tumult,
The long-journeying, cascading, hip-high urban falls.
This hydrant may be a vestige
Of a development never realized,
Unconnected to any netherworld piping.
A contractor once named the street
On which he'd built the family home
For the fiancé of his older daughter,
Abandoned later at the altar,
And for years she received mail
Addressed to Rigoberto Road.
The hydrant seems less object than symbol.
Helmet askew, his own youth gone,
My father the tillerman
Loomed twelve feet in his seat
Above the ancient cobblestones,
High enough for any New World god.

MICHAEL

Unchosen, common—
You may know several dozen—
Meaning "bearer of the word of God."

Ironic, too—I who remain
Less of a believer than you.

Proof that my mother, Ashkenazi Jew,
Knew an Old Testament moniker—
Abraham   Solomon   Isaiah—

Would seem odd in our parish.
Abe the Hebe   Ike the kike.

Better for me to be one of many:
Peter   Thomas   Luke
Stephen

And abide by my Irish
Catholic father's dictum:

Never get mad.   Get even.

PINE GROVE LODGE

Audiologists like to compare
The serene weather of the inner ear
To a swimming pool ringed with aluminum chairs,

And when your hearing begins to dim
It's as though those chairs
Have tumbled in.

August dog days 6:00 a.m.
I'd unlatch the gate to the hotel pool
Where all the chairs we'd tossed last night,

Reeking of chlorine, bright & wet,
Risen like statuary from sargasso depths,
Shed their glaze in chill Catskill air.

Little vandal, minor hooligan—
The world correcting itself as I'd slept—
I swore that, grown older, I'd attempt to hurt

No one, commit no dispassionate crime,
As my diminishing shadow stooped
Back into the cool arbor of my body

Tremoring like the hour hand of a clock
And measuring time by each muffled *thwop*
Pinecone by pinecone on the needled dirt.

MY FATHER'S COMB

When my mother insisted
  That I take *something*,
    His 5" aluminum Life-Time

Already outlined my back pocket—
  The comb I'd watched him ply
    How many thousand mornings

To rake his hair straight back
  While I waited my turn
    Before the bathroom mirror.

I wielded a 39¢ Ace hard rubber
  With a dab of Brylcreem
    To slick my mop before school,

But for years now I've run his comb,
  As he did, under the cold-water tap,
    Then dragged across my scalp

Only the shorter tines
  Of the guillotine-shaped
    Tool of vanity & work ethic.

Please take *something*, she'd said,
  My father three days dead, but
    I'd already nabbed the one object

I knew I'd touch each day
  In such casual ritual
    To comb the grief away.

TOPSY TAIL

patented by Tomima Edmark in 1991

Winter mornings, not fully risen,
Still hunched on the mattress's seamed edge,
I am there again, slumped on a distant bed,
Woozy, dream-deep, in flannel pajamas
As you shuffle, barefoot, from your room,
Sleep-flushed in a Rugrats nightgown.
With the brush you've brought me
I stroke your hair, its lush tangle,
Static electricity leaping off each bristle,
Off fingers smoothing a wayward curl,
A mini pageantry to ignite the day.
I coax light from this celestial circuitry,
The bedroom beginning to brighten,
Until hair flows along your spine,
Then slip a band onto that sparkling cascade,
Sesame open the hair above &
With the cheap pink plastic dime store tool
Loop your ponytail through that portal,
Into this 'French' style
Sweeping your neck.
                            I could almost weep
At how little it takes to make you content.
You race to the television full of cartoons
This Saturday morning thirty years ago.
I miss that light, that living
Rothko radiance, though know
Such brilliance must still exist, must
Crackle when someone else who loves you
Gathers your hair in their gentle hands.

for my daughter
on her 33rd birthday

MORNING SONG

ending with a phrase by Dugan

When I delivered my daughter to the DMV,
Don't steer *the car*, I told her,
Be the car, & after she knocked over
Six red cones attempting to parallel park,
She stormed back into the waiting room,
Sneering *Be the car! Be the car!*

All my life I have given bad advice
To those who matter most.
Marry me, I told my girlfriend.
Move closer, I urged my mother.
Write what you know, I prodded my students.
It won't kill you, I advised my late lover.

And what I didn't tell anyone was worse—
The silence offered to my father,
The praise withheld from friends.
And because when she was younger I hadn't
Taught my daughter the meaning of *aquarium*,
In her enthusiasm she raced ahead to the next exhibit,

Then the next, only to slouch back slowly,
Head down, murmuring disappointment:
More fish.
　　　　　More fish, I repeat to myself,
Sipping cold coffee before stepping outside,
Lips clamped shut, into the daily accident.

MY SON'S PENIS

Because I hear the water's white noise
But no response to his shouted name,
I open the door too soon to find him
Slipping off his briefs. Words
I'd meant to convey slip away.
I respect his privacy, so
Can't recall when I'd last seen
A penis not my own.
What surprises more than its size
Is its beauty—a tropical
Isle's unsheathed stalk, mint
Roused from winter hibernation.
My son whose voice has yet to deepen,
His goofy laughter helium-pitched,
Regards me without self-consciousness.

I had a boyhood friend whose father
Called & called him down to dinner, then
Climbed the stairs & opened the door
Onto an incomprehensible tableau:
A room illuminated by votive candles;
A boy sprawled naked upon chenille;
A jar of vaseline; a box of tissues;
A flashlight shining into a mirror
Propped against the footboard;
Marianne Faithfull ghosting up
From the spinning turntable.
Teenage masturbation
Can be such a laborious ritual.
That father shook his head, turned away.

Now I shut the door & murmur apology.
It's only a summer Saturday.
Next time he doesn't answer
Before he steps into the shower,
I promise to knock & knock
Until all the words I forgot to tell him
Come sputtering, then whooshing back.

THAT GOOD NIGHT

Do not go gentle into that good night
—Dylan Thomas

to my son
for the future

Gentle me, please, from the wheelchair,
One arm wedged under knees,
The other snaked through armpits,
Before stepping onto the square,
Brightly lit tiles to ease me
Onto the toilet seat, the air
Freshened with a spray of lilac.
Look away, please, & leave me
With a remnant of dignity
Before turning to wipe & flush,
Then gather each crumpled,
Papery part of me, this
Diminishing body, to push
Back to its narrow, semi-final bed.
I'll drift between this world
And the next where
Martin   Clara   George   Mae
Raymond   Dorothy   & all the dead
Of our not-quite-forgotten family
Claim this marrow as their own &
Together stoop to cradle me.

HOARDER

...with the first glimpse of the building, a sense of
insufferable gloom pervaded my spirit.
                                    —Edgar Allan Poe

As the memory-hoard choked the high-rise,
The elevator stuffed with boxes of mother,
The stairwells impossible to maneuver
With rags of father heaped on each landing,
I stood inside, gazing up, not ready
To clamber the oily debris.
Each apartment's a lab rat's maze: ziggurats
Of paperbacks, ashtrays, LPs.
Kitchen shelves cascade landfills of plastics
Ready to raft & drift the Pacific. Any rug
Could be the site of an archeological dig.

                    *

With each of your kisses, I discard a memory:
One punched door, one thrown dish.
I drop a face-slap down the trash chute.
With you as my lover, I ammonia light switches,
Scrub radiators of my mother's neuroses, polish
The knives of my father's affections.
I toss matches onto butane rilling the tubs
To kill any residue of familial spore.
I windex grime off six hundred windows.
Soon the high-rise will aurora the night,
And we will take over the uppermost floor.

OLD STORY

The cheaper wing in the cheap motel edged
The forest out back. Sliding glass led to patios:
Stucco walls to shield neighbor from neighbor;

A low railing to square each enclosure;
Two webbed chairs; a table small enough
For two cups weighted with wine.

Nighttime. Birds quiet, insects loud.
She undressed, knowing only the eyes
Of fox or deer could find her here,

Then pressed her navel against cool metal,
Summoning the forest forward, desiring
Its undersoul to inhabit her once more.

Air wrapped her skin in spider-silk.
She merged with the listening leaves.
Her body briefly shed all light.

When she turned, I was a stranger
Until the vision that had taken her
Diminished into sight. Wasn't I

Her lover, her tether, her familiar
Sin?—so like our forebears
We rode the night, gulping the blackness in.

THE GOOD, THE BAD & THE UGLY

1: Sunset Drive-In

Chevy Nova nosed up close,
Bree & I tilted seatbacks & gazed upward,
Not taking our eyes off the screen
As Tuco stood noosed on the gallows
While Steve & Karen fucked behind us.
Autumn '68—Karen's 16th birthday:
She wants to have a real good time,
If you know what I mean, Bree'd grinned.
High school townies. I knew what she meant,
So raffled the date among dormmates,
All of us freshmen, Steve
Promising Fireball shots all week.
Karen shone lovely in her pink dress &
When the girls dashed to the restroom
Steve kept mouthing *Holy shit!* until
They skittered back & the Civil War resumed.
Then Karen leaned forward to whisper to Bree
Who leaned sideways to whisper to me
Who turned & leaned back toward Steve
To whisper: *she wants to do it again.*

2: Kmart

Two years later, Bree & I
Long uncoupled, I hear the cashier,
Do you remember me? & look up.
Karen. Of course. How have you been?
Gone. She'd been sent away
To a home for unwed mothers run by nuns.
Gave up the baby. A boy.
Home now, living with her folks, working
On her GED. And Steve?
Flunked out, probably in 'Nam.
If you ever hear from him…
I clutch my paper sack of toothpaste,
Q-tips, condoms & disposable razors
Beyond the drab fluorescence of the store,
Then toss it into the Nova.
Twilight. November. Gold
Buried in the grave marked Unknown.
How could so many disappear?
The good, the bad & the ugly.
That Ennio Morricone score.

THE GIFT

How I wish you could watch this lizard,
  Blue now black now green,
    Scribbling the whitewashed wall:
  Living graffiti, throbbing glyph,
Shapeshifting in sunlight, feet

Splayed like asterisks,
  Little starbursts of fireworks,
    Its tail a stroke of cursive,
  Now comma now apostrophe,
As it flicks its tongue to termites.

The day is languorous, composing itself
  Slowly like these words on the wall.
    After lovemaking, you sleep
  In the sway of the mosquito net.
With your gift for making sense

Of tea leaves & coffee grounds,
  Each spill in the universe
    Never without meaning or metaphor,
  You should wake to watch this creature.
My gift would be nothing more

Than the orange skirr of a lizard
  Tagging a wall in sunlight,
    Glossed here by the man
  Who lures you with words
& with the tongue that shapes them,

Letter by letter, until you come.

for Mihaela

TABLE ON THE EDGE OF THE WORLD

Those days I would catch the ferry to Santorini
Just to sit at the table at Franco's, the table
Closest to the edge of the cliff. Barely
Big enough to hold an ashtray & glass,
Tiled & tilted & square,
It perched above the sea like a prow.
If I looked straight ahead, not at the caldera
Biding time below, I'd see
Nothing but air merging with the Aegean,
The horizon invisible, water & sky
Swirled into a primal blue boutique cocktail.
Behind me the world unfurled its cloak
As I leaned forward, unzipping the ether,
The velocity of vision speeding me
Away from the languor of my body.
Soon enough I lowered my gaze.
Donkeys hauled luggage up from the harbor,
Flies befouling their rheumy eyes.
That afternoon I read again the tattered volume
Of Cavafy, then slid it onto the shelf
Chalked **Take One Leave One**
And thumbed a book with a shattered spine,
The Confessions of Zeno by Italo Svevo, which
I rucksacked back by evening ferry
To the stone cottage & my wife's company.
Kerosene lamp. Well water.
I wondered how long we might live so simply.
I loved the novel for its quirky humor,
For its narrator's conflicted conscience
Which in its vanity mirrored my own.
Those days of the '80s have receded
Like wheel ruts below the silted seabed,

Stone roads leading nowhere
Once the volcano blackened pagan skies.
Wherever we live, some part of us dies.
Not long ago I returned to Franco's,
The bar familiar yet not the same,
As I was not the same though once again
Reading Svevo, whose book I'd tossed
Into my backpack before leaving home.
At the whim of gods
Untroubled by conscience, I finished the novel
There at that table on the edge of the world
Before returning it, damaged but intact,
To its exact spot on the shelf, itself
Imperishable down the decades,
Like the sky, the sea, the intoxicant air.

MELROSE

We named the bar Diva because we couldn't decipher
The gold Greek script stenciled on its window,
Though it may have read Maestro or even Overture
As the bar was located off Poseidonos
Across from the National Opera House.

Late afternoons, the unlit taproom empty & cool,
I'd idle on a barstool, having taught a novel
By Wharton or James, to wait for my wife
Who engaged in conversational English
With dropouts who hoped to find work in the States.

I imagined myself in love with Parthenopi,
Quick & pretty &, mainly, Greek,
Her name common, "little virgin,"
& as I sipped a second retsina
I pictured our Lawrencian life together

On her island with its homemade
Wines & edible daylilies & ringing bells
As flocks descended hillocks to sheds
Before the sun extinguished itself
In the amphora of the Aegean. *Pastoral,*

My dreamlife remained adolescent & pastoral,
& as I bided time one early dusk
The bartender, whose name I forget,
Placed a bottle of Greek gin on the bartop
Next to an empty bottle of top-shelf British,

Then slipped a white plastic funnel
Into one small mouth & began to splash
The cheap brand into the Boodles.
Seeing my surprise, he motioned
Not for you & nodded toward the opera house.

Of course. Then my wife arrived.
You must change your life, wrote Rilke, but how?
We returned home to the familiar
Arc of an American tale—but
Even now I can recall that label.

I'd purchased a bottle on our stroll home
To see how awful any gin could taste, & discovered,
Dear ex, dear reader, that it didn't burn my throat
Nearly as much as I'd thought, though
I knew I'd never   drink that gin again.

AUTHOR PHOTO

I notice first the hands: the elegant watch,
Its buttery band caressing a wrist,
The rings a glitz of fireworks—
Turquoise oval, opal circle,
Crescent of onyx.
I squint to read the titles of books
Buckling background shelves:
The fat horizontal biographies,
The slender vertical poetries.
Then the hair, upswept, brushed back,
Aura'd with sunlight
Flooding the unseen window
Where oaks must confer above eaves,
Their red leaves alive in wind.
I can almost see eggs in nests,
Webs of bagworms,
The ghostly gestures of the branches:
Forebears funneling down
The cellular debris of centuries,
Bearing histories of couplings
Until the flesh of ten thousand families
Assumes singular shape in the face.
I stare at the fixed lips, unapologetic
Nose, square chin & askew
Cheekbones, at amber eyes
Lanterned by the mind
Which composed lines
Only this poet could have written,
Then turn the book to flip it open,
Hungry for cadence, already smitten.

READING NIETZSCHE ON THE BEACH

Las Terrenas

They might be walking on water,
Those boys balanced on rubber
Soles straddling the razor
Edge of the reef where they net sardines
Flashing like silver coins
Spilled in sun.
                    If Jesus comes again,
He may not appear as a Dominican
Teen, but rather as this bent-over
Leathery grandfather
Hauling a canvas sack
Of green coconuts on his back
To sell to tourists,
Who kneels next to me
To unshoulder his burden,
Then punctures one shaven
And machete-whittled crown
To reveal the cool, clear,
And almost sweet
Water that fails to quench
This thirst to watch
Beyond my book
For any sign of divinity—
This old man
Chewing toothlessly
With so much pleasure
His jagged square
Of coconut meat, or
That teen seeming, at least
From this webbed chair,

To walk upon the sea,
Splashing lightly
Now toward shore,
His flesh above dead coral
A vertical black slash
Against the unreachable
Horizon, & waving,
He's waving back at me.

GOAT STEW

block party
Cinco de Mayo

No fan of mango or papaya, I prefer
The pineapple & banana, the less
Exotic fruits found
In markets outside immigrant
Neighborhoods. No star-shaped
Carambola dazzle those aisles, but
Here in Caribbean Food Fare
I search beyond the rust & teal
Spices for chunks of goat,
Trauma-red, heaped in mini
Pyramids below the skinned
But weird-eyed head
On glacial display. These
Knobby bits simmered
With grated ginger, root of celery,
And Scotch bonnet pepper
Will fix a stew to scent
The upper story.

Neighbors
On this street of many cultures
Cup cardboard bowls
Humped with rice
For ladled dollops of curried
Bones, then crook two fingers
To lift each piece to tongue
The strings of savory meat.
Grateful for this creature
Whose flesh stings our mouths
With the pungent taste of earth

And poverty I've never known,
We celebrate this holiday
Far from Nicaragua
Honduras   Haiti
Among strangers
Whose seasonings envelop us
In sensual camaraderie.

BRUISE

The father of a schoolmate of my son—
I don't know his name, but he's Ukrainian—
Claims that Bruce's aunt lives across the street
& swears he's seen Bruce's car parked there,
A 1960 Corvette Ragtop.
This guy knows aluminum heads & fuel injection,
290 horsepower & Powerglide transmission.
Mainly, though, he knows Bruise,
As he so respectfully pronounces the name—
The aunt in her 90s & Bruce the dutiful nephew.
Who knows what's true & what's apocryphal?
Everyone on this sandy edge of Jersey
Tells a similar tale, Bruce revving his Harley
Or posing for pics with just-married kids
Tux'd & gowned on the boardwalk.
That couple will never divorce! The dad—
His pickup wedged in the driveway, its doors
Advertising a landscaping service—points
To the house, its single blue spruce & shingle
Roof & faux redwood siding. So ordinary.
Bruise, this guy's thinking, shaking his head
At the fortune of proximity, as if the name,
The sound of a V-8 turning over, then its purr
Like an after-work sigh, still conveys
All the promise of this—how to say—bruised country.

ELEGY FOR NO ONE

Somalia. Eritrea. Burkina Faso.
Myanmar. Honduras. El Salvador.

This morning I can't unread

How the onion   the leek seller
Summoned to retrieve
The corpse of her son

Finds his head   on the soccer field
The soldiers drinking   grinning
You must take it home   they say

Carry it   through the marketplace
Following her   jeering
Are you going to make soup

She must find a box   a bucket
A secret patch of garden
Safe from scavengers

Animal / human
Who would unearth   the skull
Keep the boy   unparadised

This mother   having unslept
These many nights   unable now
To untongue prayer   her soul

Unspooling   into sky   into sea
The name of her son
Unmourned   in any history

Unchalked   on any stone

TO MARVIN

Marvin Bell 1937–2020
for Dorothy

The digital display on the bank's new marquee
7:52   8°   7:52   8°   illuminated snowfall
As I tilted into wind icing the river.
Michael! whooshed past my turned-up collar.
Iowa City, Valentine's Day, 1974.
You stood in a doorway & waved
A folder waterproofing a sheet of paper,
A poem to Dorothy,
To be printed & matted & framed
Once the art supplies store opened.
Did I want to read it? Of course.
   You are not beautiful, exactly.
   You are beautiful, inexactly.
I recognized the Shakespearean gesture
From Sonnet 130
["My mistress' eyes are nothing like the sun"],
The one that chastises poets for "false compare."
Still. A risky gambit.
              I wavered in my response.
The fleeting dots of time & temp
Reddened snow within their airy compass.
A few flakes blew onto the transparency.
We huddled together over the flame of poetry.
O, she'll love it, I told you, not lying, exactly.

ALL ORIGINAL RAMONES ARE DEAD

Catskill Poetry Workshop
1995
Larry Levis
d. 5/8/96

Familiar with each other's exes & excesses,
    We spent a week together that summer—

Your last—in Oneonta, NY, & when a woman arrived
    To spend the night with me, you imagined a fling,

Asked where I might see her again, & were surprised:
    At home— we live together.

Shaking your head, "How do you make that *work?*"
    I didn't. She was gone the following August, not quite

As you were, your presence among mountains assumed
    By Bill Matthews who limped, hips shot, cabin to class,

Amateur sommelier who would pour
    Only one summer more. Such losses.

What I loved most, Larry, was that helpless,
    Fucked-up, sad-sack humor, our laughter

As you quoted again your favorite Ramones lyric:
    I don't wanna walk around with you

I don't wanna walk around with you
    I don't wanna walk around with you

So why

        you wanna walk around

                  with me?

ELEGY WITH STRAWBERRIES

> as piliated **peck**
> the rot of shag**bark hick**ories
> —Maxine Kumin
> 1925–2014

While Max revised a poem in her study
And I eased my sore back into a chair
To read about torture in our secret war,
Mihaela & Victor drove to U Pick Em
For the season's first ripe strawberries.

Late June. New Hampshire.
Two hours later they returned
With wooden flats of cardboard pints.
We rinsed the berries & ate the dozens
While bursting juices glossed our lips

To Ruby Woo until we four
Mirrored some '70s glam rock band.
Victor, innocent of sleaze, exclaimed
Michael, your wife
Is a gymnast on her knees!

I asked Max, still swimming in her poem,
If there was a name for the device
In rhymed couplets of slanting
The final word of one line
With the internal syllables of the next.

Dipping the nippled fruit
Into its saucer of powdered sugar,
She tensed her brow in concentration, then
Yes, she grinned, pleased
With her answer: *Desperation!*

CY TWOMBLY

1928–2011
blackboard painting
1968

Staring into abstraction titled
Untitled or whose name,
Like a doorstep orphan's,
Remains secret, its ghostly

Scribbles looping darkness,
I misspoke again the prayer
Of 4'10" Sister Euphrasia, crone
Of the Sisters of St. Joseph,

Black wimple & white bib,
Creaking herself up vertebra
By vertebra to chalk
One more meek supplication.

No one could read her scrawl,
Though we dutifully copied all
Cursive into notebooks
To decipher aloud at home,

Reciting devout gibberish
Until it occurred to me
That meaning might not matter:
In her blackboard light

Of divine desire,
Our stunted nun petitioned
The Lord to allow her
To levitate into His rare

Ether, the negative weather
That suffuses Twombly's canvas,
Space   within   space   within…
Where sinners too rapturously spin.

THE LEVITATION OF SR. ALPHONSUS

Six feet tall & more, she hesitated before
The bottom metal step & tilted
Her face toward the filthy skylight,
This woman bound within
Yards of funereal drapery, bandages
To quarantine flesh from sin, who
Stood suddenly ensorcelled,
Obsidian obelisk,
                black waterfall
Reversed, her habit's hem
Rising above stockinged ankles, then
The brogues themselves lifting
A few earthly inches
As she shed her body's gravitational
Sorrow, its burdensome flesh…
Until the flushed nun
Roused herself to begin
Clanging up the school stairwell,
Ascending into fluorescence,
Once again corporeal.

TATTOO PARLOR

Kiki of Montparnasse
1901–1953

Man Ray's nude image of Alice Prin—
Shot from behind, a studio portrait,
Seated & turban'd & vamping the lens,
Her hourglass torso inked with the f-holes
That spill siren song from the violin—
Blues my forearm; the needle chirrs.

Expressionist moonlighting as model,
Prin signed self-portraits
     Kiki —
And who wouldn't reinvent themselves
By gazing within, then marking that change
On paper
   or canvas
      or hiring this nipple-
Pierced headbanger to stipple a swatch of skin?

NUDE

Even your mother wouldn't believe
That you'd posed for the portrait
Tacked like an icon above our bed.
She admitted no likeness, failed
To see a single aspect
Of your anatomy, not rucked
Scar or tattooed amaryllis, though
You'd unbuttoned your dress,
Slipped off underthings,
To freeze—to hold fast—
In the studio's high-watt heat.
You'd wanted a classical rendering
As though you'd been whisked
From the past, from the aesthetic
Flowering of antiquity,
Flesh transmuted from marble—
One of three graces
Unshackled from her pedestal—
Your likeness meant to be
A gift for this year's anniversary.
Arms tucked behind waist, fingers
Clasping wrist, toes splayed,
You lifted your chin,
Ostriched into your pose, then
Allowed the eager
Student artist to begin.
Sheryl Crow on the stereo.
He pinched the charcoal stick
&, line by line,
Curve by slender curve,
Began to stroke
The contours of your hips,

Staring, sketching, then staring
More intently until he assumed
Unearned familiarity
With the freckled,
Hieroglyphic
Intimations of your body,
& read beckoning into each
Stipple & fleck.
Sweat beaded your navel,
Your upper lip,
& bones shifted their rickety
Scaffolding under skin.
Modeling was such hard work.
Then he attempted to fill in
The features of your face, but
Desire outpaced skill,
Your nose obscured by thumb-
Smudge, mouth a crooked slash,
One eye wildly
Misshapen, any vestige
Of singularity gone.
Only breasts & slitted sex
Blossomed clearly, darkly,
Beneath the rippled
Waterfall of your hair.
The finished portrait
Depicted almost every
Woman in anonymous
Solidarity with so many
Thousands
Pinned to studio walls,
Weighted with stones on flea market
Tables, undone on easels
Propped in life drawing classes—
Still, despite the artist's amateurish
Gaze, despite his helpless

& voyeuristic
Infatuation,
I often glimpse the grace
You'd wished to channel
Each morning when we awaken.

SELF-PORTRAIT WITH BANANA

When the Studio Arts professor
Assigned still lifes of a single object,
I chose the banana for its shape & color,
But too quickly the banana
Turned, during the days of my drawing,
From green-going-to-yellow
To daffodil
To fulvous egg yolk
To speckled trout
To oil spill
As the black bottomknot crept upward,
Blotting the fruit,
Seeping beyond its sorry skin
Over the serene interior scene—
Tablecloth, bowl, blank brick wall—
As I sketched again & again
The spoilage, the relentless rot,
Until forty black paper sheets
Windowed the walls of my house,
Each a study of willful rejection
Of the things of this world &
All that they are not, each
A mirror of failure, each
My veil, my shroud,
My darkling cloud,
Each my final
Erasure.

COUNTDOWN

It's not the tunes, though as I grow older
Oldies are what I growl & yammer,
Now to myself, though years ago
I crooned those relics to my daughter
In our woozy, casual
Bedtime ritual. *In the Still of the Night.*
Earth Angel.
        It's not the stories,
Though several seem original,
Perfectly formed fictions
In three-minute articulations.
It's not their endless repetitions,
Or nonsense syllables sung
With the thrill of giving over
To Pentecostal tongues or
The fervor of sexual rapture,
Nor their poor grammar,
Lopped-off *g*s & unsaintly *ain't*s,
Not even their wildly
Misbegotten similes:
You keep my heart jumpin' like a kangaroo
Floatin' like an onion in a bowl of stew.
It's their unselfconsciousness:
Isn't this how we've longed to speak
Our affections—in artless couplets
Flung from lips, with ardor
Spun from top-forty hits
Whose rimshot beats still pulse our hearts?
Twilight Time. There's a Moon Out Tonight.
I wail oldies as the countdown starts.

EASTER ELEGY

1927–2022

Deepening into dementia, my mother
Mistook the flowering bush behind me
For a sleeping bear.
                                    It's only forsythia,
I calmed her. Look:
Yellow. Four-lobed. A brief bloom.
Still, what does a son know?
A cool breeze joggled the boughs.
If that bear wakes up, I'm outta here!

SHARK RIVER BRIDGE

That spot in the center of the bridge
Where the seam splits metal, where
The two leaves of the span part
For tuna boats—their 7' rods
Rigged high as though trolling for God—
That spot above the gray waters of the inlet
Where Avon-by-the-Sea arcs into Belmar—
That's where I'll jump some wintry predawn
Once dementia has commenced, before it seeps
Deeper into my brain & swerves me
From my purpose, protects me from self-harm,
Makes my death dependent
Upon those whose love will stay their hand.
I'll wear my black woolen overcoat, its pockets
Jangling with silverware, & wash down
With a tumblerful of vodka
The long-amassed tablets of Ambien
Before leaping toward oblivion.
Watching our elders deepen into dementia,
We rehearse escapes, our exit fantasies.
I will not gaze like my mother beyond the son
Who visits the memory care facility, will not
Pluck incessantly a ghost-hair off my tongue
Or spin & spin again the buttons of my cardigan
Only to focus suddenly on his face & whisper—
Those glinting hooks descending—"I want to kill you."
No. I will not.   I've picked my spot.

PRAYER WITH CARAVAGGIO

I will no longer enter a cathedral
Unless it conceals a single
Caravaggio
In a recess reeking of incense
Where one bulb illuminates the oils
That they may shine more darkly,
That I might recognize the human
Flaws in divine depictions
& weep with wonder.
I'd rather stroll the local mall,
The galleria in Milan
Where women burdened with bags
Stop to scratch with one foot
The bull's huge balls for luck.
That mosaic on the tiled floor
Snorts near sliding-open doors
Where summer's dense, ungodly heat
Hammers the falsely frigid air,
While prayers exhaled for centuries
From nearby pews in candled naves
Diminish in the vaulting.
Here is my prayer, murmured over ice
Shaved into a paper cup
Euro'd from a vendor
At the bottom of these cathedral
Steps where I sprawl, syrup
Sweetening my tongue.
I will no longer enter a cathedral,
But wherever I go
I'll still pray with the sinful
Devotion of Caravaggio

Who paid his prostitute, robed in blue,
To pose for a tableau
As the poxed yet holy
Virgin Mary.

OCTOBER MAPLES

When faith begins to fail, to fall away
Like jawbone flesh turned floppy jowl,
I watch my slow mixed lab
Devour gizzards spooned into her bowl,

Lick the fulsome hand in gratitude,
Then circle phantom grasses
Before slumping onto the rug to paw
Her grizzled, grease-streaked snout.

Against the deviltry of fleas
She whimpers an improbable bible.
Sleek once more in dreams, flouting laws,
She preens before a clique of yipping spaniels.

Open the door: the devout dog will stay
Despite a lawn alive with squirrels.
When faith begins to fail, to fall away,
Look to the mongrel who suffers you,

Unlike those lithe, social, doomed
& unleashed strays
Racing beyond their numbered days
Along gold-flecked, leaf-strewn avenues.

OLD DOG

Look: unclipped nails
Score for purchase the tiled floor:
They clack & claw: a sad cartoon.
I give her one more gentle tug.
Her scraggly coat's a drab rag rug:
Her spine slumps like a churchyard plot.
Her final litter weaned & gone,
This lab's a crumpled paper bag.
I can't bear to see her beg, so heap
A bloody bowl of chicken hearts
To stain her snout. I watch her slowly eat.
I lead her slowly out.
Dog years/human years: our bodies age
By any measure of loss. Listen:
Old whore, old queen, your dry teats
Sag & sway & sweep the pollen
Off the floor. I recognize
My shrunken self within your rheumy eyes
& rage before the quivering tip of tail
Grown hairless, mottled, & obscene.

SINNERMAN

> Oh, sinnerman, where you gonna run to?
> —traditional African American spiritual

First you see only shadows, sable bristles
   Stippling the silty, ribbed floor, then
      Glimpse the suspended apparitions.

Pencil-long, glassine so almost invisible,
   Needlefish swept by my shadow
      Quickly stitch tropical shallows.

How can creatures so sleek & barely real
   Inscribe pure presence through still,
      Colorless, estuarial pools?

My noon shadow folds absence into my body
   Like black rice paper origami,
      Then steals slowly outward at sunset,

A darkly famished silhouette
   Whose hunger nothing can fulfill.
      This sinnerman inhabits me.

No wonder the needlefish flee.

NEEDLEFISH

Platybelone argalus

Almost invisible & ludicrous,
This purely horizontal needlefish

Must have shimmied at the final moment
Through creation's clenching orifice.

As wheels of icy nothingness
Swirled closer before forever fusing shut,

One last slash of celestial light
Wriggled through that minuscule hole:

Imperfect, unfleshed, & spectral,
My shadow's sister: a soul.

RED-BILLED FIREFINCH

Lagonosticta senegala

Birds called pithis, sold…across Senegal for a dime…
are believed to carry away sins when set free.
                              —*The New York Times*

I whisper sins into empty birds,
Then set them free. So many sins, pithis
Untold. I watch them wing the sins away.

I buy finches from vendors in makeshift stalls,
Exotics in cages like sins in souls,
Touch lips to plumage where ears must be,

Then flick my finger to let each bird loose.
Have you seen my sins, scarlet flocks wheeling,
Unbound from my body? Have you witnessed

Modest comets arcing trees, feathery
Fireballs of forgiveness, plump pithis
Looping back now to hook claws within me?

CARROT

Blessed be sin if it teaches men shame.
—Georges Benanos
Diary of a Country Priest

This clod-caked taproot tugged from soil
Then rinsed in water clear & cool

Flares like a soul made visible
By sin that's seen as good once gone.

The world consists of there/not-there.
I choose between each one each hour.

I eat the carrot raw & whole
From tawny tip to fronded crown.

I eat the carrot   not the soul.

ANXIOUS ECLOGUE

Ios

That morning was one of several dozen
When, having woken as the sun
Broke over sparse brown hills,

I paused in geography so elemental
It might have composed itself
Centuries ago: gray scrub, gray shale,

A donkey roped to a low stone wall,
The pale shore beyond, & beyond that
The blue-laden bowls of water & sky.

Then who was I in this imperishable
Reverie?—a breathing bone pile,
Wobbly sundial, tongue-tied oracle,

Shepherd who'd lost his wooly flock,
Sinner who'd burned the family bible.
I unstrapped my sandals to mark

Footprints on the path to the well
Where the viper uncoiled its spine,
Briefly spilling my shadow

As I stepped over the creature
To whom I'd grown familiar.
Through its narrow, yellow eye-slits,

In the merciless light of this country,
I'd become inconsequential,
& no more damned than any donkey.

EATEN BY BEAUTY

Dominican Republic

The yellow-crowned night heron
Plucks the land crab
Inching from its burrow,

Cracks its red shell
To pick with whetted beak
The shredded innards.

The heron's plumed skull
Shaded gray & black
Seems rendered by Caravaggio.

How holy to be eaten by beauty,
Or to scuttle
Under a thistle to pinch

The green & blue
Iridescent beetle
& allow beauty to inhabit you.

LAST WORDS TO MY SOUL

after Hadrian

Go, little sister,
Flesh flap peeled
From blistered heel,

Yellow pellicle
Skimmed with a fork
Off scalded milk.

Where will you go,
How far on wind-whistle
To marrow within a creature

Not yet born
When I become no longer
Your bodied brother?

Vanishing twin, forever young,
No reason to mourn
As beetles unfasten my tongue.

NOTES

The dedication quotes a phrase from "Stump" by Mihaela Moscaliuc in her book *Cemetery Ink* (University of Pittsburgh Press, 2021).

The epigraphs are taken, respectively, from "Hawthorne and His Mosses" (1850) by Herman Melville & "Gloria" by Van Morrison in the version by Patti Smith on her album *Horses* (1975). Smith's lines are not Morrison's but adapted from her poem "Oath."

"All Original Ramones Are Dead": for Marcia Southwick, with admiration across the decades.

"Carrot": the epigraph by Georges Benanos is one of his "beatitudes" in *Diary of a Country Priest* (1936).

"Countdown": corresponds with "About Opera" by William Meredith.

"Elegy with Strawberries": the epigraph is taken from "Where I Live," a poem written in rhymed couplets, in *Where I Live: New & Selected Poems 1990–2010* by Maxine Kumin (W.W. Norton, 2010). Thanks to Martyna Dobkiewicz for introducing me to the name of the lipstick.

"Hoarder": the epigraph is taken from "The Fall of the House of Usher" (1839) by Edgar Allan Poe.

"Last Words to My Soul": according to the *Historia Augusta*, Roman emperor Hadrian wrote the poem beginning "animula vagula blandula" [little soul little wanderer little charmer] on his deathbed in 138 CE.

"Lone Hydrant": for Angela Ball, with admiration across the decades.

"Michael": corresponds with "Give Your Daughters Difficult Names" by Assétou Xango, which corresponds with "The Birth Name" by Warsan Shire. The poem also recalls, for better or worse, Gertrude Stein's remark about Ulysses S. Grant in *Four in America* (1947): "It is the first or Christian name that counts, that is what makes one be as they are."

"Old Story": "the undersoul…precludes all but a generative concept of Eternity, a concept based in propagation, thereby confirming a pagan disposition." —John O'Loughlin, *Terminological Dictionary of Social Transcendentalism* (Centretruths Digital Media, 2014).

"Pine Grove House": for Don Schofield.

"Red-Billed Firefinch": epigraph: "Absolution, With a Wing and a Prayer" by Jaime Yaya Barry, *The New York Times*, October 5, 2016. These finches are also known as "birds of forgiveness."

"Sinnerman": versions of the African American spiritual have been recorded by Nina Simone, Peter, Paul & Mary, & Sinéad O'Connor, among many other artists.

"Tattoo Parlor": I'm grateful to Stephanie Tobia for arranging my first visit to a tattoo parlor, Skin City on Ormand Quay Lower in Dublin. The tattoo based on Man Ray's photograph of Kiki of Montparnasse was inked at Electric Tattoo in Asbury Park, NJ.

"That Good Night": corresponds with "Do not go gentle into that good night" by Dylan Thomas.

"To Marvin": the two italicized lines open (in regular font) "To Dorothy" by Marvin Bell. In "Poetry Is a Manifestation of Life: Talking with Marvin Bell" by Emily Sernaker in *The Rumpus* (March 23, 2018), Bell is asked how the poem came about: "It was 1976 in Iowa City. Christmas was coming, and I wanted to write a poem to her, which I have often done for Valentine's Day...." However, the poem first appeared in August 1976 in *The Atlantic*, so it had been written earlier. Although memory is imperfect, I'll stand by the date in the poem.

"Window": corresponds with the poems of Hadara Bar-Nadav in *The New Nudity* (Saturnalia Books, 2017).

ACKNOWLEDGMENTS

Warm thanks for their generous support to the editors & staffs of the journals & books in which these poems, sometimes in earlier versions, appeared:

Alaska Quarterly Review: "Reading Nietzsche on the Beach," "Topsy Tail"
America: "Sinnerman"
The Arkansas International: "Melrose"
Arts & Letters: "Anxious Eclogue," Needlefish," "Pine Grove Lodge"
Barrow Street: "October Maples," "Cy Twombly"
Bennington Review: "Morning Song"
The Christian Century: "Carrot," "Eaten by Beauty"
Copper Nickel: "Prayer with Caravaggio"
The Florida Review: "Bruise," "Old Dog"
Gargoyle: "Michael," "*Window*"
The Georgia Review: "Red-Billed Firefinch"
The Gettysburg Review: "Nude"
The Hopkins Review: "Brooklyn Walk-Up"
J Journal: New Writing on Justice: "Elegy for No One"
Miramar: "All Original Ramones Are Dead"
Nine Mile: "Author Photo," "Countdown," "Table on the Edge of the World"
Ploughshares: "Last Words to My Soul"
Plume Poetry 10: "To Marvin"
Poetry Northwest: "Elegy with Strawberries"
Salt: "The Good, the Bad & the Ugly"
Southern Indiana Review: "My Father's Comb"
Stone Canoe: "Easter Elegy"
This Broken Shore: "Tattoo Parlor," "The Levitation of Sr. Alphonsus"

"Red-Billed Firefinch" appeared in *Caw* (BOA Editions, 2020).

"Self-Portrait with Banana" appeared as a limited-edition letterpress broadside from Blue Satellite Press at Millikin University in Decatur, Illinois; the poem also appeared online, in *Live Encounters Poetry & Writing* (Ireland).

"The Gift," "The Levitation of Sr. Alphonsus" & "Melrose" appeared in *Live Encounters Poetry & Writing* (Ireland).

"Shark River Bridge" appeared in *Sign & Breath: Voice & the Literary Tradition*, eds. Philip Brady & Shanta Lee Gander (Etruscan Press, 2023).

"My Son's Penis," translated by Teodora Coman, appeared in *Poets in Transylvania*, eds. Radu Vanca, Ştephan Baghiu, Vlad Pojoga & Dragoş Varga (Sibiu, Romania, 2022).

Gratitude to the administrators & staff of the Virginia Center for the Creative Arts for the 2021 residency that allowed me both time & space in which to deepen into these poems. Special thanks to Sheila Pleasants.

For their various kindnesses, conversations & correspondence, I remain grateful to Michael Broek, Elena Karina Byrne, Edward Hirsch, John Hoppenthaler, Ilya Kaminsky, Gerry LaFemina, John Lucas, Terry Lucas, Shara McCallum, Laura McCullough, Ron Mitchell, Alicia Ostriker, Suzanne Parker, Carl Phillips, Boo Poulin, David Rigsbee, Harold Schechter, Maurya Simon, Elizabeth Spires, David St. John, Sholeh Wolpé &, especially, Judith Vollmer.

Thanks too to Philip Brady & Robert Mooney & the generous & meticulous staff at Etruscan Press for their warm & enthusiastic welcome.

Kiernan & Fabian, you prod me always to be my better self through your own examples. Zach, welcome! Mihaela Moscaliuc, our life together remains a wonder.

In fond memory of Gerald Stern (1925–2022)

A NOTE ON THE AUTHOR

Michael Waters has published numerous books of poetry, among them *Darling Vulgarity* (BOA Editions, 2006), finalist for the *Los Angeles Times* Book Prize, & *Parthenopi: New & Selected Poems* (BOA Editions, 2001), finalist for the Paterson Poetry Prize. He has edited/co-edited several anthologies, including *Border Lines: Poems of Migration* (Knopf, 2020) & *Contemporary American Poetry* (Houghton Mifflin, 2006). Recipient of five Pushcart Prizes, fellowships from the National Endowment for the Arts, the John Simon Guggenheim Memorial Foundation, & the Fulbright Foundation, & Individual Artist Awards from the Maryland State Arts Council & the New Jersey State Council on the Arts, he lives without a cell phone in Ocean, NJ.

Books from Etruscan Press

The Confessions of Doc Williams & Other Poems | William Heyen
The Football Corporations | William Heyen
A Poetics of Hiroshima | William Heyen
September 11, 2001: American Writers Respond | Edited by William Heyen
Shoah Train | William Heyen
American Anger: An Evidentiary | H. L. Hix
As Easy As Lying | H. L. Hix
As Much As, If Not More Than | H. L. Hix
Chromatic | H. L. Hix
Demonstrategy: Poetry, For and Against | H. L. Hix
First Fire, Then Birds | H. L. Hix
God Bless | H. L. Hix
I'm Here to Learn to Dream in Your Language | H. L. Hix
Incident Light | H. L. Hix
Legible Heavens | H. L. Hix
Lines of Inquiry | H. L. Hix
Rain Inscription | H. L. Hix
Shadows of Houses | H. L. Hix
Wild and Whirling Words: A Poetic Conversation | Moderated by H. L. Hix
All the Difference | Patricia Horvath
Art Into Life | Frederick R. Karl
Free Concert: New and Selected Poems | Milton Kessler
Who's Afraid of Helen of Troy: An Essay on Love | David Lazar
Mailer's Last Days: New and Selected Remembrances of a Life in Literature |
J. Michael Lennon
Parallel Lives | Michael Lind
The Burning House | Paul Lisicky
Museum of Stones | Lynn Lurie
Quick Kills | Lynn Lurie
Synergos | Roberto Manzano
The Gambler's Nephew | Jack Matthews
The Subtle Bodies | James McCorkle
An Archaeology of Yearning | Bruce Mills
Arcadia Road: A Trilogy | Thorpe Moeckel
Venison | Thorpe Moeckel
So Late, So Soon | Carol Moldaw
The Widening | Carol Moldaw
Clay and Star: Selected Poems of Liliana Ursu | Translated by Mihaela Moscaliuc
Cannot Stay: Essays on Travel | Kevin Oderman
White Vespa | Kevin Oderman
Also Dark | Angelique Palmer
Fates: The Medea Notebooks, Starfish Wash-Up, and overflow of an unknown self |
Ann Pedone, Katherine Soniat, and D. M. Spitzer

Etruscan Press Is Proud of Support Received From

Wilkes University

Youngstown State University

Ohio Arts Council

The Stephen & Jeryl Oristaglio Foundation

Community of Literary Magazines and Presses

[clmp]

National Endowment for the Arts

Drs. Barbara Brothers & Gratia Murphy Endowment

The Thendara Foundation

Founded in 2001 with a generous grant from the Oristaglio Foundation, Etruscan Press is a nonprofit cooperative of poets and writers working to produce and promote books that nurture the dialogue among genres, achieve a distinctive voice, and reshape the literary and cultural histories of which we are a part.